Character For Kids

Character For Kids

Devotions and Activities for Kids Ages 3–10

By

JOHN G. GAGE

Illustrated by Becky Noia

RESOURCE *Publications* · Eugene, Oregon

CHARACTER FOR KIDS
Devotions and Activities for Kids Ages 3–10

Resource Publications
An Imprint of Wipf and Stock Publishers
199 W. 8th Ave., Suite 3
Eugene, OR 97401

www.wipfandstock.com

PAPERBACK ISBN: 978-1-7252-5719-1
HARDCOVER ISBN: 978-1-7252-5720-7
EBOOK ISBN: 978-1-7252-5721-4

Manufactured in the U.S.A.   FEBRUARY 11, 2020

Johnggage.com
Cover design by Rachel Gage

Contents

Illustrations

The Bat—**Sharing**

The Mouse—**Adaptability**

The Prairie Vole—**Loyalty**

The Dolphin—**Sensitivity**

The Beaver—**Persistent**

Preface

I HAVE FIVE PRECIOUS grandchildren: Tanin, Alhanna, Coral, Cailee and Clara. My goal for each of them since they first came into this world has been to see them adopt Biblical values that would make them kinder siblings, more responsible students, loyal citizens and committed Christians. I must say here their parents are doing a fantastic job and I am not sure that they *need* more input from "Gampa."

These devotionals are meant to be read by mom and dad to their kids, and then discussed. I would take one trait per week and let your child (children) find ways through the week that each trait could be practiced and applied to their own lives.

The activity pages are intended to give your child a "hands-on," enjoyable way to remind them of the animals that illustrate each character trait. *Be Creative*! They can color, draw, complete, whatever they desire. The idea is for them to experience something that will remind them of the character values we (you) want them to remember.

When my oldest daughter was three years old, we were in the local country store, which was owned by a friend. He had given her candy on occasion, but on *this* day she decided to help herself to the candy, which was handily displayed at her eye level. When we discovered this "infraction" we took her back to the store, had her return the candy to the owner, and apologize for taking the sweet treats without permission. You have stories like this too! Hopefully this book will help in our efforts as parents, grandparents, teachers and mentors to instill positive values in those little ones that we love so much. Soli Deo Gloria!

Drawing is Fun

You will need a pencil, some paper, and a good eraser. Don't worry if your drawing doesn't look like the one you're using as an example.

Most animals start with circles, ovals, squares and triangles.

Try to figure out which shapes to use and how big to make them.

We'll start here with just the face. You can try the whole animal if you want.

Next, you need facial expressions. First try only straight lines. For the eyes.

Now you'll need a mouth.

Noses are pretty easy.

Ears come in all sizes and shapes.

Courage Verse

"Be strong and courageous . . . for the Lord your God is with you wherever you go." (Joshua 1::6–9)

Courage

The Lion

A GROUP OF LIONS is called a *pride,* and every pride has a leader. This leader can be a boy or a girl and is chosen because of their courage and strength. The roar of a leader lion can be heard up to five miles away. The roar of the leader makes all the lion's enemies afraid, and this protects the pride from being attacked.

The Bible character Joshua was chosen to become the leader of Israel after their first leader, Moses died. God told Joshua, *"Be strong and courageous . . . for the Lord your God is with you wherever you go."* (Joshua 1: 6–9).

Courage means "the ability to keep on going, even when faced with danger or difficulty." It doesn't mean that you will never be afraid, but it *does* mean that you can face every day with confidence, because God is *always* with you. He will protect you, and He will provide everything that you need.

Courage means placing your hand in God's strong hand and letting Him lead you. You can face any challenge because God is with you.

To draw a lion's face, start by drawing a square.

Next, draw a triangle on the bottom of the square.

Now erase the line connecting the triangle and the square.

Add a mane, ears, and face.

Color the 3s light yellow. Then, color them again with light brown.
Color the 2s brown.
Color the 1s red.
Do not color the eyes unless you just want to.—Choose any color or combination of colors for the blank spaces.

Caring Verse

"Let Him have all your worries and cares, for He is always thinking about you . . ." (*TLB*)

Caring

The Elephant

ELEPHANTS ARE THE LARGEST animals in the world, and they spend up to sixteen hours a day eating! (Maybe that is why they are so big!) They are very good swimmers, and they have the largest brain of any animal, and are very intelligent!

When an elephant is stressed or afraid, another elephant will touch his face with his or her trunk and make a high- pitched chirping sound (a little bit like the sound a bird makes) to help calm the one who is upset.

The grown-up word which means "to care for someone else" is the word "empathy." That means that when someone else is sad or afraid, you *feel* that emotion and try to help make your friend feel better. Sometimes the best comfort is just being with them when they are lonely, afraid or sad. Sometimes you can encourage them with a Bible verse, pray with them or just cry with them. When a friend is going through difficult times, it is a great help to know that someone cares about them and wants to share their burden.

God does that for *us* when we are hurting. I Peter 5:7 says, "Let Him have all your worries and cares, for He is always thinking about you . . ." (TLB). When we are sad, lonely, afraid or feel ignored, God sees us and comforts us. He loves you very much, and wants you to know that He is always close to you, and ready to help carry your burdens.

We all want to act toward others like God acts toward us. He is our best example. So, when someone close to you is going through a hard time, show them that you care by being available to help them, just like God is available to you.

How many words can you make using only the letters in the word:

E L E P H A N T ?

2-letter words   3—letter words   4-letter words

5-letter words

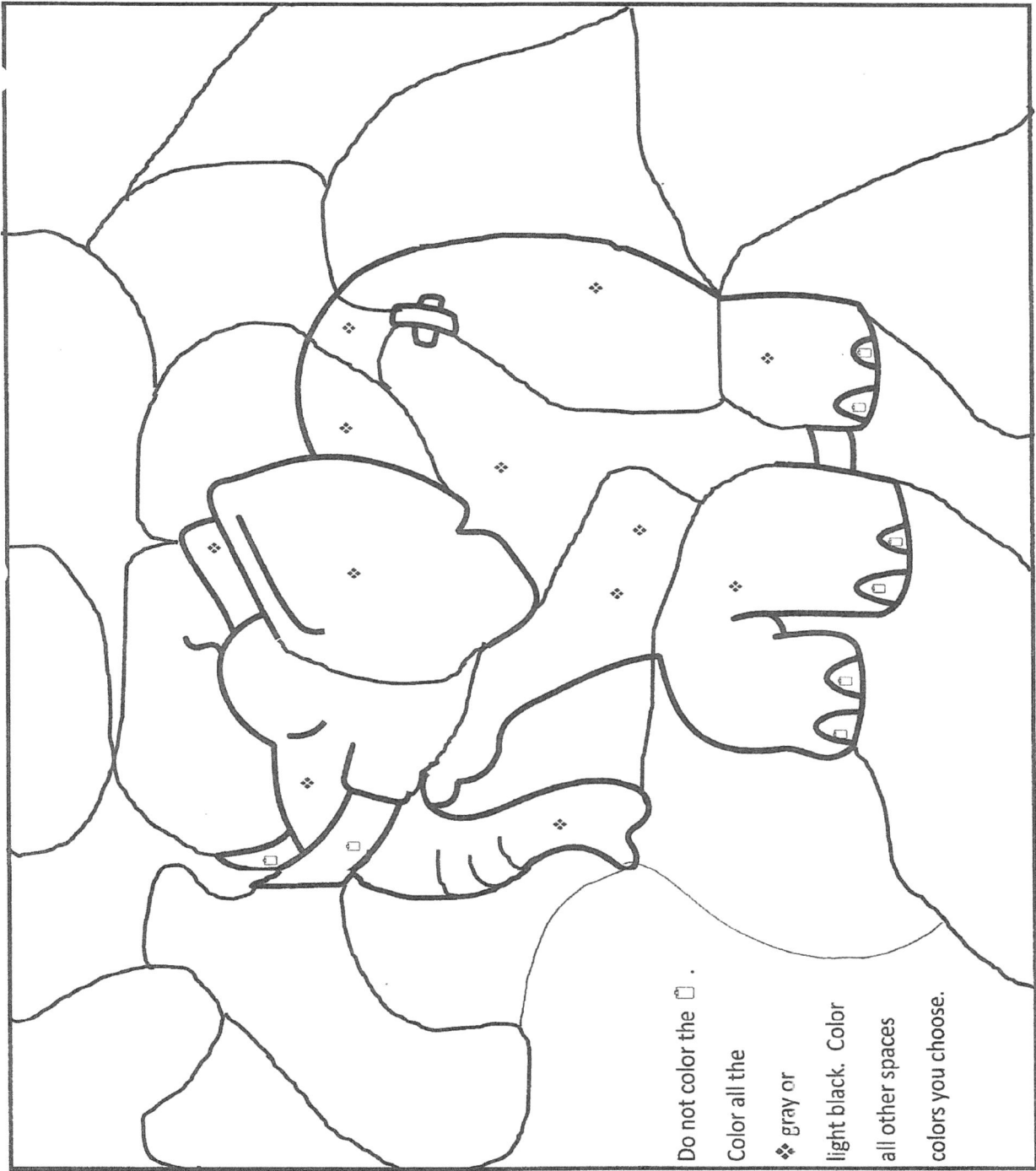

Do not color the ▢ .

Color all the

❖ gray or

light black. Color

all other spaces

colors you choose.

9

Respect Verse

"Show proper respect to everyone, love the family of believers . . ." (1 Peter 2:17)

Respect

The Camel

THERE ARE TWO TYPES of camel . . . one type has *one* hump, and the other type has *two* humps. The camel stores up food in their humps so they don't have to eat as often as other animals. God made them to live in the desert . . . they have an extra eyelid which protects them from blowing sand, and they can go a long time without water because of the water storage in their humps. Camels can carry up to six-hundred pounds of weight, which is a *lot* of weight. When a person wants to get on a camel and go for a ride, the camel has to *kneel* so that the rider can get on! (See if you can find a picture of a person riding a camel!)

Kneeling is usually a sign of respect. A person always kneels when they are in the presence of royalty, like a king or queen. Kneeling shows that we understand that the other person has authority over us, and we are letting them know that we humbly bow when we are in their presence. That is why it is a good idea to kneel when we pray! It shows that we realize that God is in charge, and we are approaching *His* presence with humility and submission to His will.

Respect means thinking and acting in a way that shows that you care about other people and their feelings. It means that your treat others as though they are important, because they are! It means that you are willing to let the other person go first, or you obey your parents because you respect the fact that they are older and wiser than you are. Respect means recognizing the value of another person.

1 Peter 2:17 says, "Show proper respect to everyone, love the family of believers . . ." Have a "kneeling" attitude toward others, showing them that they are valuable!

Word Search

Find words about the camel. You can find words left to right or top to bottom. Some words appear more than once.

```
P  A  C  K  Q  B  S  N  B  Y
A  L  X  C  R  O  A  S  I  S
L  M  U  A  D  W  N  E  T  A
M  H  U  M  P  D  D  C  R  R
T  P  R  E  S  P  E  C  T  E
R  D  E  L  G  J  S  K  K  S
E  S  S  O  K  N  E  E  L  P
E  A  P  V  S  P  R  A  Y  E
V  F  E  E  T  I  T  D  E  C
M  M  C  R  E  S  P  E  C  T
W  A  T  E  R  R  R  I  D  E
```

Word list

BOW, CAMEL, DESERT, FEET, HUMP, KNEEL, LOVE, OASIS, PACK, PALM TREE, PRAY, RESPECT (4 times), RIDE, SAND, WATER

How many differences can you find between the 2 camel pictures?

13

Commitment Verse

"... A friend loves at all times ..." (Prov 17:17)

Commitment

The Dog

THE DOG IS THE most committed animal on earth. Since they are so loving, they become attached to people and remain with that person for life. One dog named *Hachi* met his owner at the train station every day after work. After the owner suddenly died, Hachi continued to meet the train for nine years, even though his master was gone!

Commitment means "doing what needs to be done regardless of your talents or mood." (The Smart Playbook). It means being willing to keep your promises . . . if you make a commitment or promise to clean your room, you keep at it until your room makes your Mommy proud of you! When you are committed to your family or friends, you support them and encourage them when they go through times of sadness or trouble.

Proverb 17:17 says, " A friend loves at all times." This means when your friend makes a mistake, you are still their friend. When they don't treat you nicely or they take something from you, you may not like the way they have *acted*, but you are still their friend. Being committed to someone does not depend on their behavior, it is a promise that *you* make to remain committed to them no matter what. Just like Jesus stays committed to you even when you mess up.

Drawing a dog's face

Dogs can be difficult to draw.
They range in size from 2 pounds
To 150 pounds. Their ears can be
Tall and pointy, floppy and long,
short and stubby. Their tails can
be long, short, fluffy, curled.
They can have curly fur, straight fur,
Short or long fur. They can be
Brown, black, white, spotted.
It's easy to understand why it can
be difficult to draw a dog.

A fun way to start is to put your
thumb on a piece of paper. Bend
your thumb and trace around it.

Add details to make it any kind
Of dog you want.

Help the dog find his things.

LOVE

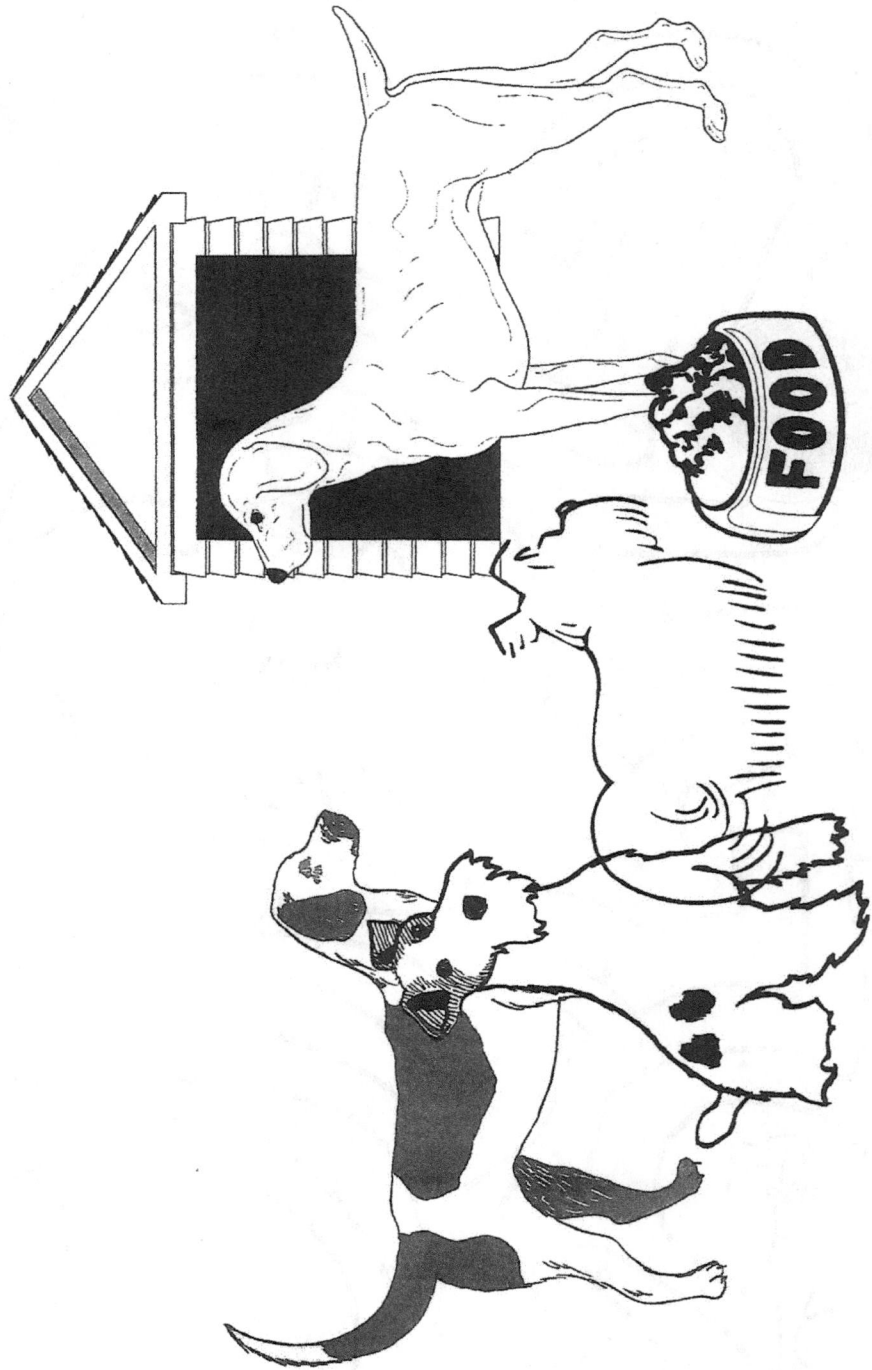

Being Observant Verse

" As the deer pants for water,
so I long for you, O God." (Psalm 42:1; *TLB*)

Being Observant

The Deer

DEER LIVE IN "HERDS." The male deer, called a "buck" grows antlers so he can protect the herd, while the female deer, or "doe" takes care of the little deer, called "fawns." Deer have eyes on the sides of their heads, so they can see *almost* all the way around without turning their heads. If you watch a deer carefully you will notice that they nibble on some grass for a little while, then lift their heads, their ears go straight up, and they notice what is going on around them, looking for any movement that might mean danger.

Being observant is noticing what is happening around you. If Mommy is feeling a little stressed, you notice that and try to help her with the chores. If Daddy is very busy you notice that and try not to get in his way until he is finished. If a friend seems sad, you notice that and try to comfort them. Being observant is *looking*, and *listening*, like the deer, so you know what is going on around you.

The Bible says, " As the deer pants for water, so I long for you, O God." (Psalm 42:1-*TLB*) The deer is always looking for water, because water keeps them healthy and strong. A wise person is always wanting to know more about God and how to live for Him, because that keeps a person spiritually healthy and strong. We learn more about God by going to church and Sunday School and *listening* very carefully, and by having Mom and Dad read Bible stories to us, and by *watching* how followers of Jesus live their lives. When we watch and listen carefully, we are being observant, and then, like the deer, we will grow stronger and wiser, and our lives will make Jesus happy. I hope that Y*ou* are learning to be observant . . . just like the deer!!!

Can you find:

a carrot    a ball   a pencil   a paper clip   a candle

an envelope   an orange slice   a kite  a ruler

a crown   a bone   a button    a party hat

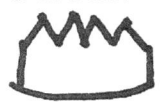

DOE

FAWN

BUCK

LISTEN

DEER

WATCH

OBSERVE

22

Self-Control Verse

"It is better to have self-control than to control an army." (Proverbs 16:32)

Self- Control

The Chimpanzee

THE CHIMPANZEE IS AN interesting little animal! They live in "families," and eat mostly figs, certain leaves, and . . . are you ready? TERMITES! Chimps are very smart . . . *so* smart that they are willing to give up a small treat now for a bigger treat later on . . . and *that* is called Self-control.

Self-control is the ability to say *no* to something good now, so that you can have something even better later! For instance, if Mom offers you *one* marshmallow *now*, or *three* marshmallows if you will wait an hour, then waiting, which takes self-control, is better! If playing outside looks like fun, but you need to do some schoolwork, it is better to get the schoolwork done now, and play *later*, when you can play *longer* without worrying about having to finish your work!

Self -control means telling yourself *no*, which sometimes can be difficult, but is a wise choice if waiting leads to something even better!. Sometimes when we are trying to decide what to do, *waiting* a while before we decide will help us make the correct choice. Self-control is the ability to control your choices without being told what to do by someone else . . . when you can delay what you want now for something even better later on, it means that you are growing up!!

Proverbs 16:32 says, "it is better to have self-control than to control an army." In other words, the ability to *wait* for something is better than being physically strong, and better than being in charge of a lot of people. You can't control anyone else, but you *can* control yourself! That is called *self-control*!

Drawing a Monkey

To draw a monkey, start with a circle and an oval.

Add 2 ovals for the legs and 2 small ovals for the feet.

Now, begin to use your eraser to get rid of lines you don't want. Remember, you can always add lines back in if you erase the wrong one. When your drawing looks the way you want it to, add some arms. Remember, a monkeys arms are very long.

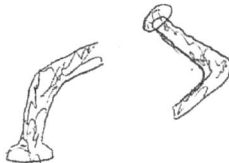

Do you want your monkey to stand?

Give him 2 ovals for each leg.

Don't forget the 2 small ovals for his feet.

If you want, you can add fingers and toes.

Remember, a monkeys hands and feet

look very much alike.

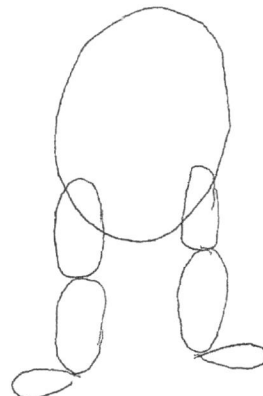

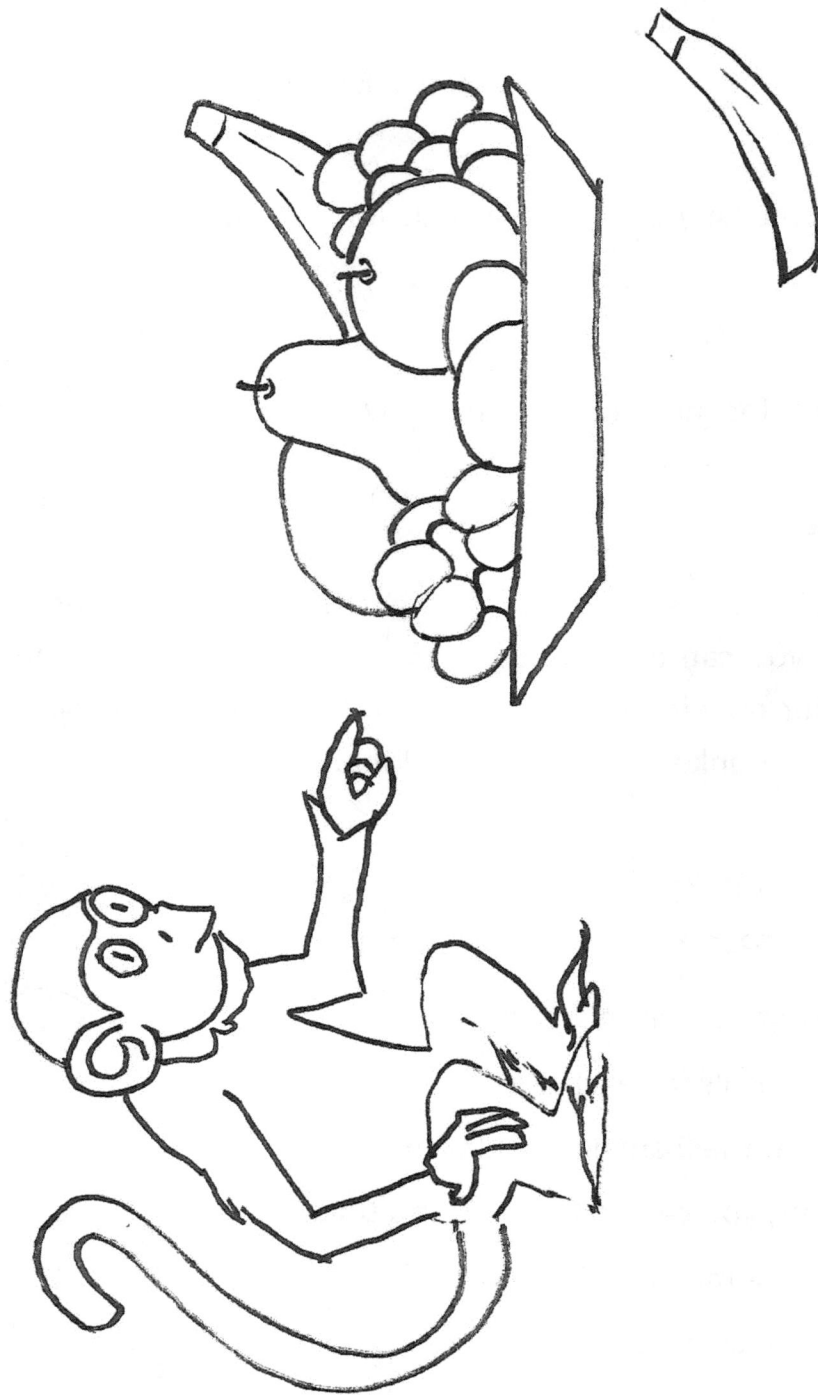

Hard Work Verse

" Go watch the ants, you lazy person. Watch what they do and be wise." (Proverbs 6:6)

Hard Work

The Ant

ANTS LIVE IN FAMILIES called colonies, and every ant has a specific job. Ants are very strong and can carry up to fifty times their body weight (which is like *you* carrying your family car around the neighborhood!!) Ants build underground homes with many rooms, all connected by tunnels. They work very hard to build their homes and then protect them. You never see a lazy ant . . . they are always busy and always helping their friends build their homes.

We all need time to relax and play, but we accomplish a lot when we are willing to work hard. That means that when there is a job to be done, like cleaning your room or finishing schoolwork, it is good to stay at it until the job is finished. If we don't finish our work now, we will have to come back later to complete our job. You might as well work hard now to finish your assignment, so that you can play later without worrying about completing your job later.

Proverbs 6:6–8 says, " Go watch the ants, you lazy person. Watch what they do and be wise. Ants have no commander . . . no leader or ruler, But they store up food in the summer and gather their supplies at harvest." That means that ants work hard to finish their jobs without having to be told what to do. They work because it is the right thing to do, not because someone is making them do it.

Be like the ant! Work hard at the jobs that you need to do, and then you can enjoy some free time without worrying about a job that needs to be finished. When you work hard, you accomplish a lot and make others proud of you!!!

Every ant has an identical twin (not necessarily the same size.)

Can you find the twins?

Help the ant find its home.

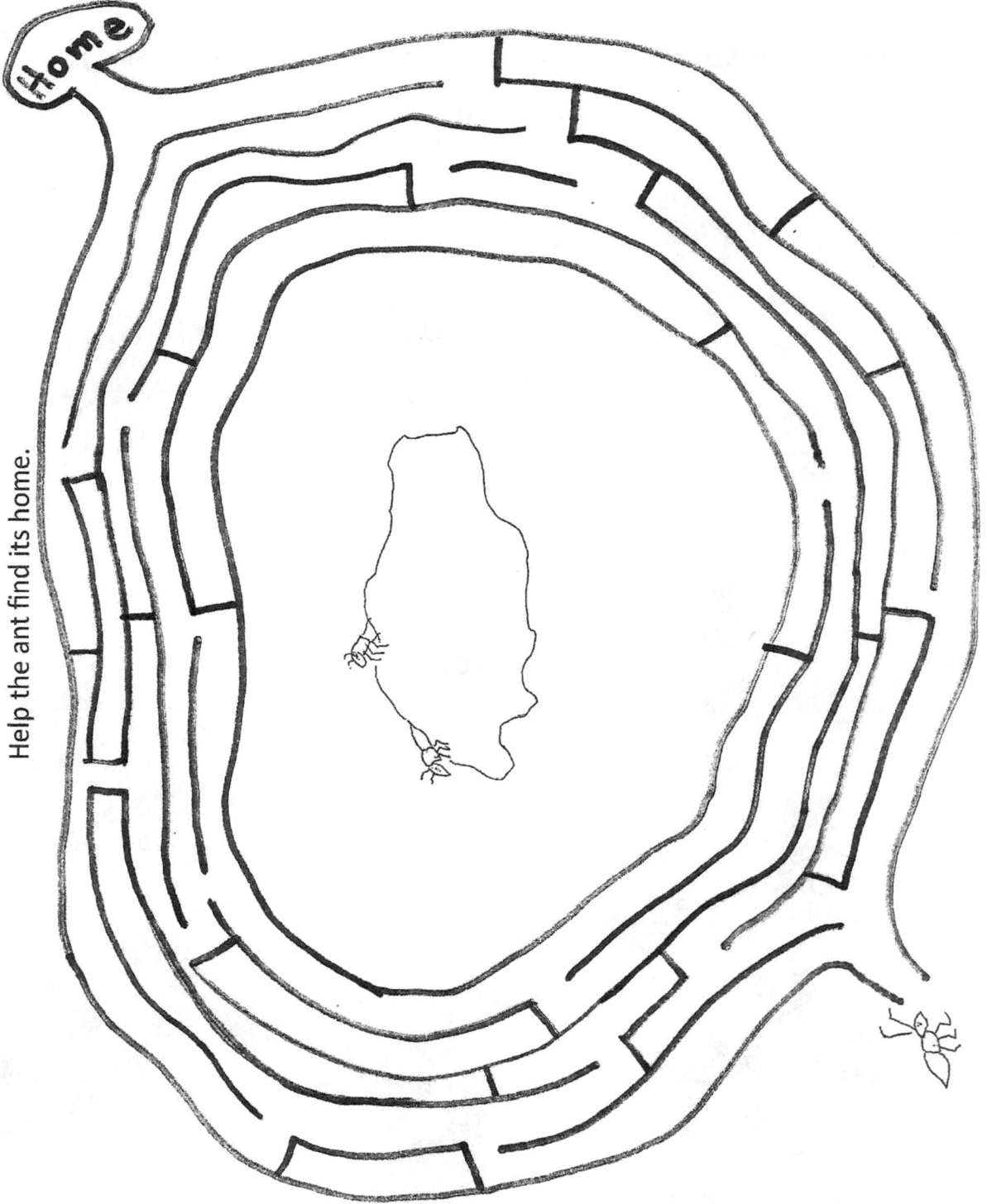

Manners Verse

" Do to others as you would have them do to you." (Luke 6:31)

Manners

The Raccoon

HAVING GOOD MANNERS MEANS behaving in a proper way while around other people. The raccoon is a great example of an animal with "manners." They wash their hands before a meal, and they wash their faces with their feet, just like a cat. When they eat they sit up and hold their food in their hands (because raccoons don't have silverware!!)

Manners for *people* include things like saying "please" and "thank you," not interrupting when others are speaking, asking permission before doing something, not commenting on the way other people look, knocking on closed doors before entering, being respectful of others and never making fun of anyone. People with good manners cover their mouth when they sneeze or cough, hold doors open for others and offer to help Mom and Dad around the house.

The Bible talks about having manners! In Luke 6:31 we read, " Do to others as you would have them do to you." Sometimes we call this the "Golden Rule," but it really is a lesson on manners, being respectful of others, and treating others in the same way you want others to treat you. Work at remembering to use good manners . . . and people will enjoy being around you because you treat them respectfully!

Something is missing from each raccoon.

Please draw the missing part.

Sharing Verse

"No one felt that what he owned was his own; everyone was sharing." (Acts 4:32; *TLB*)

Sharing

The Bat

THE BAT IS AN interesting little fellow! When you think of a bat you probably think about the make-believe vampire, but bats don't live in coffins, they live in caves in very large families called *colonies*. They have a very well- developed sense of hearing and can tell how big an object is, how far away it is and how fast it is moving, all in a split second! They like to eat insects, so it might be handy to have some bats hanging around your house! Bats have been known to eat up to twelve-hundred mosquitos in an hour!!

One very interesting fact about the bat is that they love to share! They want to make sure that every bat in their colony gets enough food, so they share generously with bats in their immediate families and with bats from other families. When one bat shares with another, they have found that the bat who receives the gift of food often repays the giving bat by sharing with *them* when they are in need!

The word *share* means to let someone else use your portion of something. For instance, if you are playing with several toys that belong to *you*, sharing means allowing brothers, sisters or friends to play with them too! At mealtime sharing means to evenly distribute the food so that everybody gets some, rather than one person getting a lot, and the others getting a small portion or nothing. Sometimes it means letting someone else have the last piece of pizza, or the last piece of pie! True sharing means dividing the last piece so that everyone gets some of it!!

The early church knew how to share. Acts 4:32 says that, "no one felt that what he owned was his own; everyone was sharing. (*TLB*)" These Christians learned that the best way to make sure that everyone had enough was to share. And that is good advice for *all* of us!

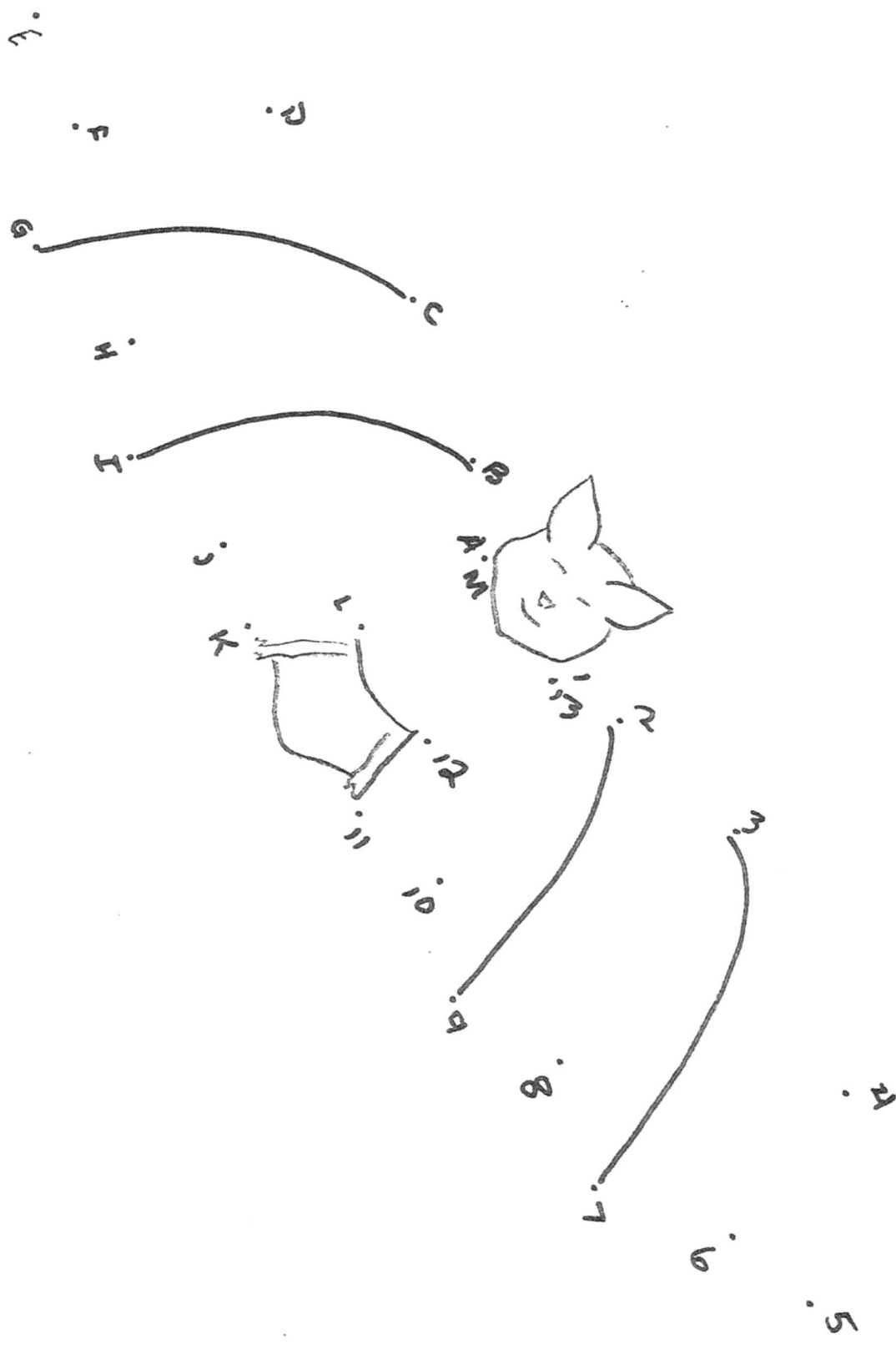

A <u>bat</u> can <u>fly</u> at <u>night.</u>

Find the pictures that rhyme with the underlined words. Then, see how many more rhyming words you can think of.

Bat	Fly	Night

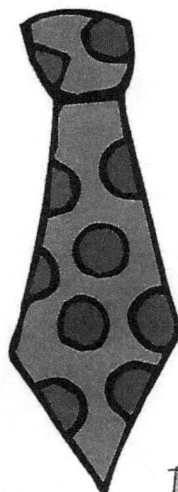
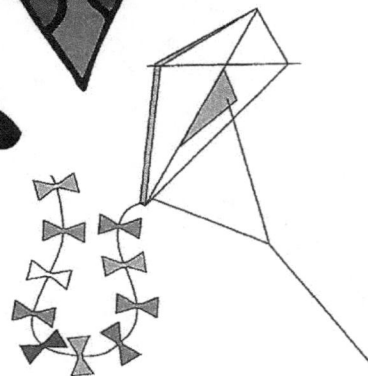

Adaptability Verse

"I have learned to be content whatever the circumstances." (Phil. 4:11; *NIV*)

Adaptability

The Mouse

THE MOUSE IS A cute little animal, but we don't like to see them in our houses!! A group of mice is called a "mischief"! The mouse can adapt to living anywhere . . . in walls, attics, basements and under floors. Many of them live in fields and make nests underground. They can jump up to a foot and a half, will eat anything, and never stray more than a few feet from their homes. They are also very neat: they have one area of their nests for eating, one for using the bathroom, and another for sleeping!

To be able to adapt means to feel comfortable in different situations. It is the ability to change in order to fit in different circumstances. If you change schools, you need to be able to adapt to new teachers and new friends. If your family moves, you need to be able to feel comfortable in a new home or a new neighborhood. If you have a baby brother or sister, it's important to welcome them to your family and adapt to those new circumstances.

The Apostle Paul learned to adapt. He said, " I have learned to be content whatever the circumstances." (Phil. 4:11; *NIV*). Paul was happy talking to one person or talking to a crowd.. He was content when he had money and when he didn't. He learned to adapt . . . just like a mouse!

Mice are hiding on this page. How many can you find?

Drawing a mouse

A mouse has big, round ears. Walt Disney decided that, no matter which direction Mickey was facing, his ears would always be facing the same direction. That was smart. It made Mickey much easier to draw.

A mouse also had a pointed nose and a long skinny tail.

Sometimes, it's fun to use the most

Obvious characteristics of an animal,

And let your imagination add the details.

If you want to draw the body of a mouse,

Follow the directions for the vole and give it a long tail.

Loyalty Verse

"Never let go of loyalty and faithfulness . . ." (Proverbs 3:3 *GNTA*)

Loyalty

The Prairie Vole

THE PRAIRIE VOLE IS related to the mouse, and looks like a hamster, but they live in the desert in underground tunnels. They eat mostly plants, and communicate by the way they stand: for instance, when they feel threatened, they push their head forward, raise their front feet and chatter their teeth.

The most interesting fact about the Prairie Vole is that they find one partner and stay with that partner for life. This is called loyalty. They care for their young together, build their tunnels and nests together, and protect their nests together.

Loyalty is being faithful to a person or an idea. If you are loyal to a friend, you will help protect them and remain friends even through difficult times. If you are loyal to the teachings of the Bible, you will obey what Go says to do, even when others are doing something different.

Proverbs 3:3–4 says, " Never let go of loyalty and faithfulness . . . If you do this, both God and people will be pleased with you." (*GNTA*) You can show loyalty by keeping your commitments, helping those in need, serving others and encouraging those who are hurting. You can show loyalty to your parents by being obedient and helpful.

One way to draw a prairie vole:

First, draw a rectangle and a triangle.

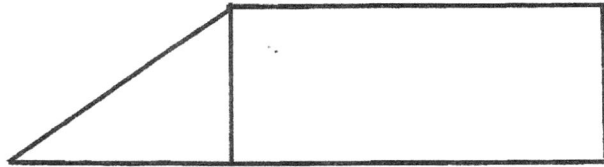

Next, erase the line connecting the rectangle and the triangle.

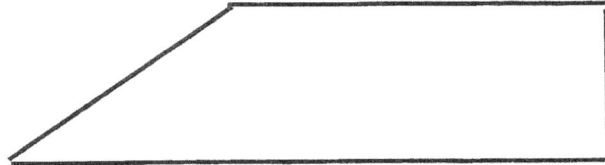

Now, add the face, fur, and other details. You could also give him some grass to hide in. If he's hungry, you could also add some nuts or berries to eat. How about drawing a friend to share with?

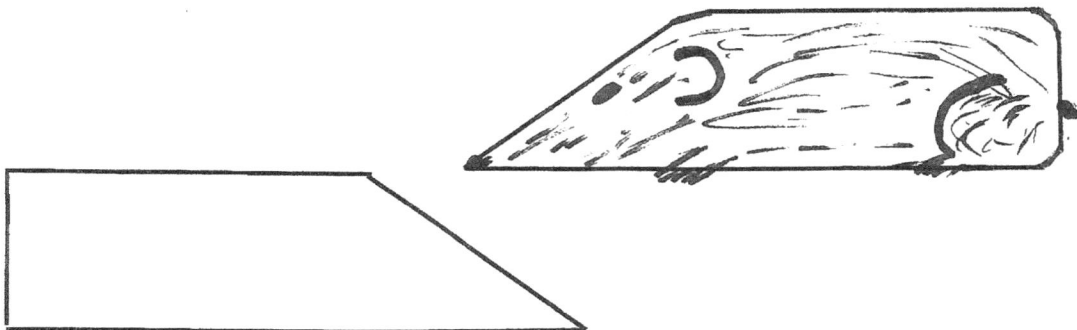

Compare the two pictures. How many differences can you find?

Sensitivity Verse

" A sensitive answer soothes anger." (Proverbs 15:1 *NIV*)

Sensitivity

The Dolphin

THE DOLPHIN IS ONE of the world's most intelligent creatures, and also one of the most sensitive. They know when another dolphin is in pain or is stressed, and they communicate encouragement through a unique "whistling" sound. Dolphins can see very well, even in muddy water, and have a highly developed sense of hearing. They also enjoy touching one another, and they have wonderful memories, recognizing dolphins they haven't seen in a long time!

Sensitivity is being aware of the feelings of other people. When someone is sad, that makes us sad too, and we want to cheer them up. When someone is happy, we smile with them. When someone has been hurt, we want to help make them feel better. In other words, we are "sensitive" to the way others feel.

Proverbs 15: 1 says, "A sensitive answer soothes anger." (*NIV*) When we are aware of the feelings of someone who is unhappy, and can respond gently and kindly, it makes things better. When an angry person knows that you understand the way they feel, the anger gets smaller and smaller. It is always wise to be aware of the feelings of other people, and to try to help them when they are going through tough times. Be like a dolphin . . . be aware of the feelings of others!

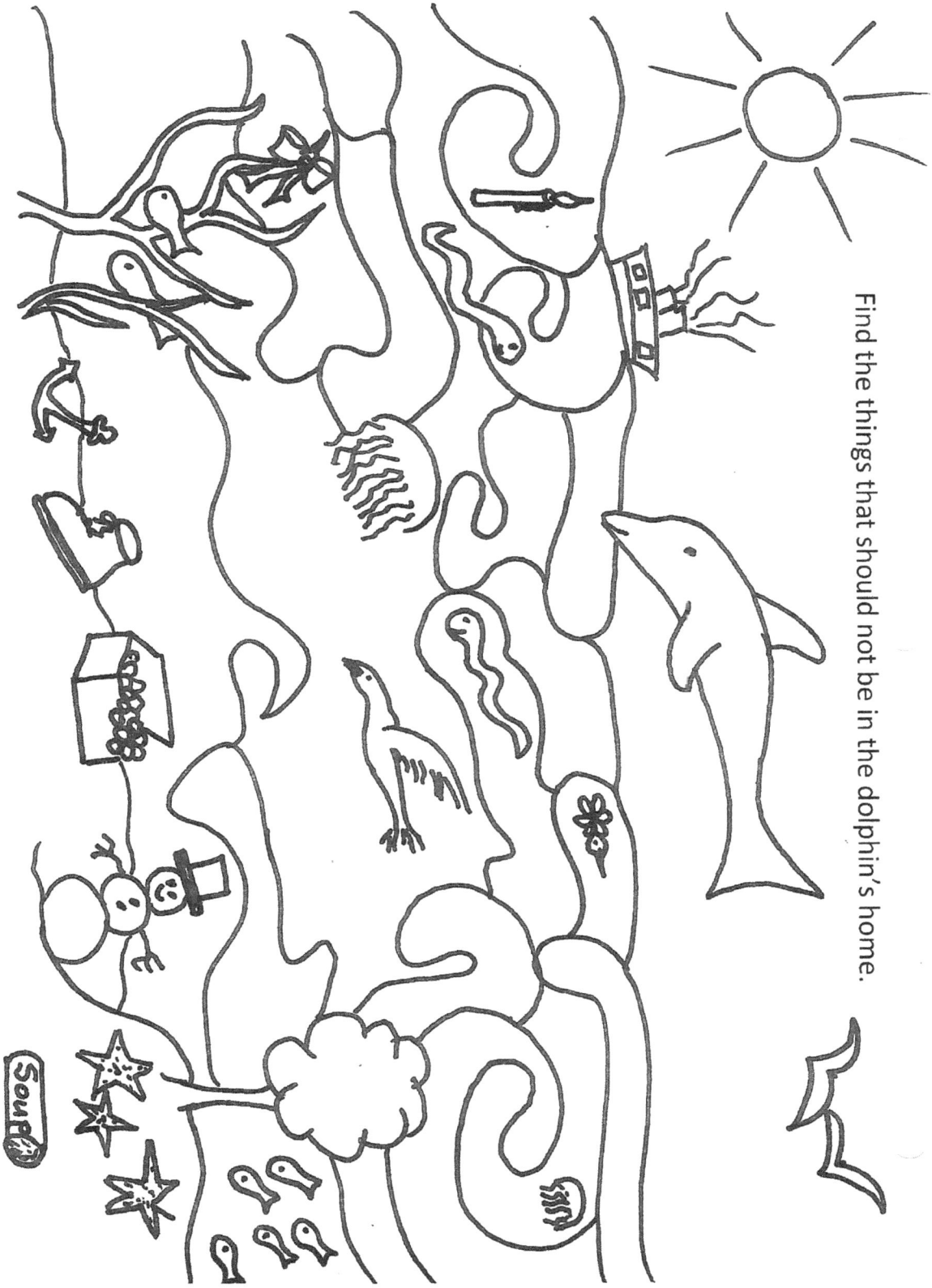

Find the things that should not be in the dolphin's home.

Persistence Verse

" Be persistent and you will finally win." (Proverbs 25:15 *TLB*)

Persistence

The Beaver

BEAVERS BUILD BIG WALLS in the water called "dams." Since beavers are safer in water than on land, they use these dams to stop up pools of water where they can escape from animals that want to hurt them.

After beavers choose a location for their dam, they work tirelessly, for days and weeks to build it, and nothing can stop them from finishing their job! These huge wood walls can be up to two-thousand feet long and eighteen feet high (Ask Mom or Dad to explain how big that is!!) They use their flat tails to help them sit and swim, and to warn others of danger. They chew through big trees with their sharp teeth and then roll the fallen trees to the water.

Persistence means to keep at a job until it has been finished, even when that is very difficult. It means never giving up, but to continue to work hard until your job is complete. That could be something you do to help Mom around the house, or school homework, or helping Dad build something. You just keep at it until you have finished what you started.

Proverbs 25:15 says, " Be persistent and you will finally win." (*TLB*) So don't give up until the job is finished, just like the beaver!!

How many animals do you see that begin with the letter "B?"

Can you find any animals that do not begin with "B?"

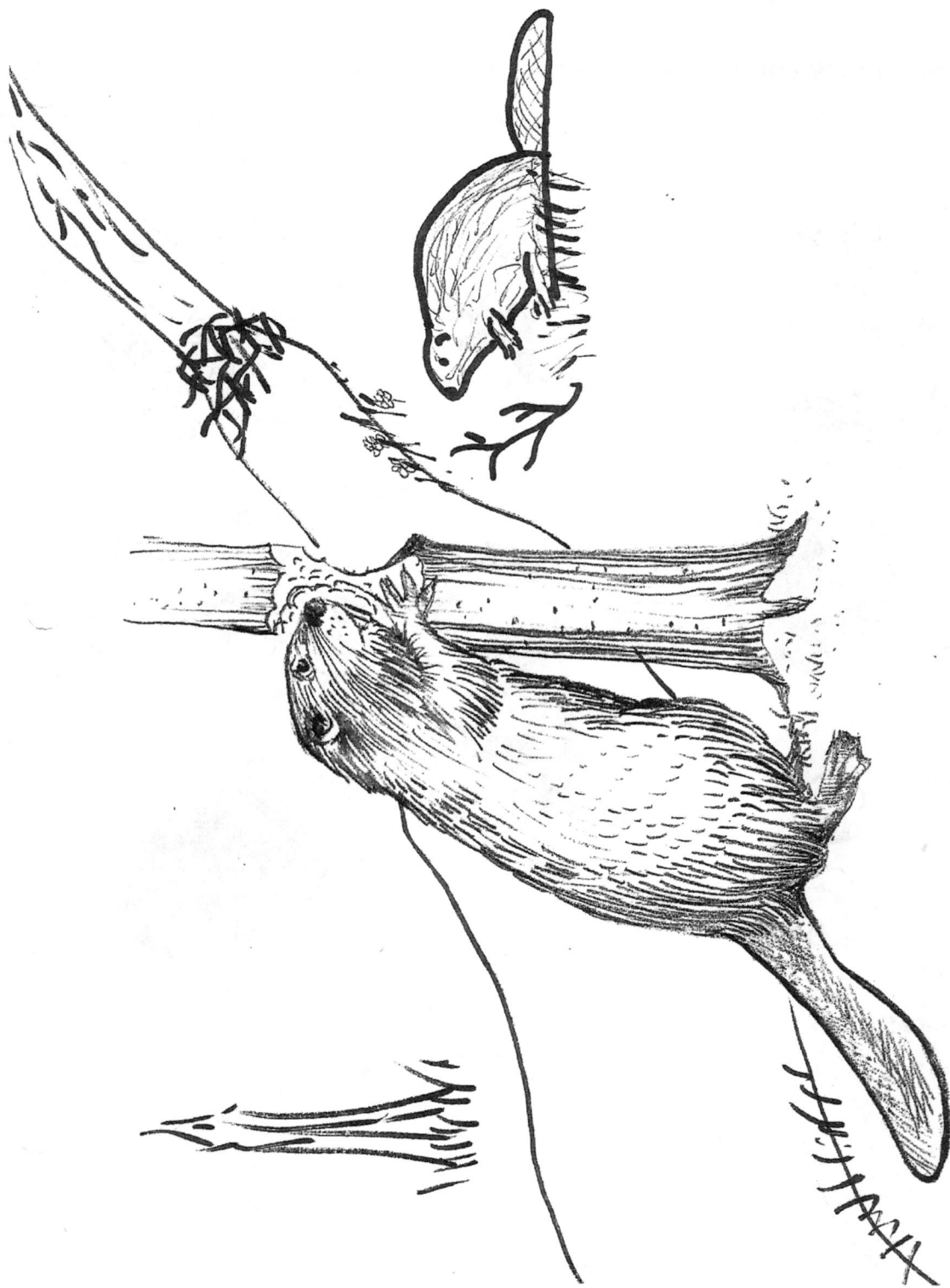

www.ingramcontent.com/pod-product-compliance
Lightning Source LLC
Chambersburg PA
CBHW081341090426
42737CB00017B/3236